Volume and Market Profile Trading

Unlocking Profitable Paths: A Comprehensive Guide to
Mastering Volume and Market Profile Trading Strategies for
Financial Success.

Abraham Robert. C

When you purchase volume and market profile trading book, you will gain exclusive access to our complementary video course, absolutely free!

(FIND LINK TO THE VIDEO COURSE AT THE END OF THIS BOOK)
Claim your gift today and take the first step towards success in your trading journey

TABLE OF CONTENT

Chapter 1

Important of volume and market profile

Market Profile Easily Identifies Market Value

It is tremendously beneficial for a trader or investor to know and appreciate where value is in the market compared to the present market price when buying or selling any financial instrument. Market Profile can be used to find both long-term and short-term value in the market. Market profile is the only charting approach capable of identifying market value for any currency pair.

It identifies key levels of support and resistance.

Investors and traders benefit greatly from the three-dimensional picture of market movement and the capacity to organize market data in a normal distribution pattern. A vision that standard charting techniques cannot provide.

The profile chart's support and resistance levels are determined by real market activity and value criteria. Market profile help traders to identify key support and resistance levels more readily and consistently.

Distinguishes between trending and non-trending markets.

Any currency pair in the Forex spot market is constantly shifting between states of balance and imbalance. The profile allows you to track the currency's balance points as well as market movements between balance and imbalance. The development and course of movement of the profile quickly reveals the presence of a directional trend or a sideways market. As a result, directional motions may be captured early in their development. A trending market's profile structure is narrow and lengthy, but a balanced market's structure is more developed and broader.

Assists Traders in Projecting and Forecasting Price Targets

Market profile charts, as a general concept, shift our attention away from price. The profile incorporates the market value notion into its research, forex markets function like any other market system, influenced by supply and demand dynamics. Any currency market fluctuates between periods of balance and turbulence. The market develops around a fair price when prices strive to discover a new value area following each trend. When there is an increase or drop in purchasing, prices shift out of equilibrium, and prices trend upward or lower until a new equilibrium is reached. The rules of supply and demand govern the whole price-setting process.

This dynamic is readily evident on the profile chart, allowing for exceptional accuracy in forecasting range expansions and prospective price goals.

Identified trade opportunities

The profile is a one-of-a-kind graphic depiction of the market. The form and structure of the profile help traders to detect and pinpoint trading opportunities that would not be visible on any other chart.

Market Profile Offers Structural Protective Stops

Many beginner forex traders find it difficult to choose an acceptable spot for a safe stop. Most times beginner traders are often stopped out of a trade only to have the market shift and move in the favor of their trade after they have been stopped out.

The profile structure allows a Forex trader to choose and fix protective stops on important structural area. This enables traders to choose protective stop placements strategically and correctly for each transaction. The proper placement of a protection stop minimizes possible losses and improves the risk management process for each transaction. Check the practical session chapter for more explanation.

It's basically an innovative and intelligent method of analyzing the Forex market.

Unlike standard technical analysis and charting approaches, which merely monitor price movements using technical indicators, Market Profile theories give the trader with a plethora of information about the market's underlying structure and strength. A trader can obtain a far better grasp of market activity and the market factors driving it by using the power of the profile.

Market Profile Trading

Market profile trading is not simply another financial analysis tool; it is a game changer. Beginner and expert traders may use a variety of charting methods and tools to monitor markets and price activity. A market profile is one instrument that may give more precise measurements of market performance. Understanding what a market profile is and how to understand it will help you execute trades more efficiently.

Market profiles are essential because they allow traders to better monitor and anticipate the accumulation and dispersion of various markets. Using this information, traders may be able to place trades more successfully and have a better knowledge of how each market operates on a daily basis.

Investors may find that market profiles help them learn to utilize simpler volume charts more efficiently, since studying market profile charts may be more complicated but still needs a fundamental understanding of how trading charts function.

Volume in Forex Trading

Volume in forex refers to the number of lots traded in a currency pair over a certain time period. In other words, the quantity of cash purchased and sold. Volume signifies relatively little on its own, but when combined with price action and momentum, it may indicate whether or not trends are likely to continue.

Volume also refers to a market's liquidity, or how quickly currencies can be purchased and traded. When there are more traders on the market, you have a better chance of opening and closing positions swiftly and with a reduced spread. The main forex pair have the biggest volumes, resulting in the most liquidity.

A low-volume pair has less liquidity since fewer traders purchase and sell the currency. This is often the case with minor and exotic forex pairs.

Volume profile

Volume profile is an additional trader's tool that allows you to identify the crucial levels that major market participants consider while trading. It is sometimes referred to as horizontal volume.

This tool's worth stems from its ability to be coupled with nearly any trading strategy. After studying the market using horizontal volumes, you will have a more trustworthy signal that can be utilized to confirm or reject the received entry point.

The volume profile is shown on the chart as a level scale.

With their assistance, you may discover the price at which market participants performed the greatest number of transactions.

The strongest and most important level is easily identifiable visually. It will be symbolized by the longest bar.

Distinguishing between Volume and Market Profiles techniques

Although the terms Volume Profile and Market Profile are sometimes used interchangeably, they have different techniques for market analysis. Here is a breakdown of the two profiles:

The Volume Profile techniques

The Volume Profile technique visualizes trade volume vertically at different price levels.

It identifies high and low trade activity, as well as support and resistance levels.

Volume Profile places less focus on time-based analysis than Market Profile.

Market Profile techniques

TPOs are created to show traded price ranges over particular periods by integrating price and time.

It provides a comprehensive knowledge of market dynamics by analyzing the correlation between price levels, volume, and timing.

Chapter 2

The basic of volume

Volume trading in forex involves trading currency pairs with substantial buying or selling pressure. It can assess the strength of a market trend and provide optimal entry opportunities for traders.

The concept of volume

Volume in forex refers to the total number of currency pairs exchanged in the market over a certain period of time. The number of units exchanged determines the volume of the currency pair, and vice versa.

• High volume during an uptrend suggests a strong bullish trend, prompting traders to put long orders.

- Higher activity during a decline suggests a strong negative trend, prompting traders to put short orders.
- Low volume during an uptrend suggests a weak bullish trend leading to a negative reversal, prompting traders to put short orders.
- Lower volume during a downtrend suggests a weak negative trend leading to a bullish turnaround, prompting traders to put long orders.

Factors to Consider when trading volume

Trend strength

When currency pair prices continue to rise, they show a strong upward trend, indicating that there is a high level of buying interest in the currency pair. This, in turn, results in higher volume transacted by buyers, signaling market continuance.

On the other side, when markets are choppy and do not follow a certain trend, it indicates that the volume being traded is low, and markets may reverse.

Price Reversals

When the market has been in a specific trend for a long time and begins to see an opposite movement in prices while the volume remains high, it suggests a substantial likelihood that the market may reverse.

Bullish candle sign

A bullish candle indication may imply strong buying pressure. This suggests that the volume is rising, and a strong bullish trend may continue in the near future.

Bearish candle sign

A bearish candle indication may imply strong selling pressure. This suggests that the volume is rising, and a strong bearish trend may continue in the near future.

Breakouts versus fake breakouts

When a price breakout occurs during a current trend and volume falls, it suggests a larger likelihood of a fake breakout and advises traders to hang on to their positions. The true breakout happens when the currency pair's values break above or below their present levels with increased volume.

Volume history

Traders may compare the volume traded now to the volume traded for a currency pair in the previous one to five years or lesser depending the type of trader. The more recent the data being compared, the better the possibility that future volume predictions are right. If recent data reveals a large volume, traders should place orders in line with the current trend; if recent data shows a dropping volume, traders can trade against the trend after doing a proper structural analysis.

Forex Volume Trading Strategy

Trend trading volume strategy

Trend trading volume strategy

Volume may assist traders who like to follow the general direction of movement by establishing whether a trend has begun before jumping in - rather than opening a position only to discover it was a false signal.

Most pro traders prefer to see more volume in order to get in on a trade, since it implies that the market is moving with vigor.

If the price moves up (or down) without increasing volume, it may indicate a lack of momentum and a reversal.

Reversal trading volume strategy

Reversal trading volume strategy

Some traders deliberately seek prospective reversals in order to anticipate and profit from a shift in opinion.

If, after a lengthy upward or negative trend, the price begins to vary in smaller price movements but still has a big volume, it may suggest that a reversal is likely. This is because price swings demonstrate that neither the bulls nor the bears have total control of the market.

So, if you detect a reversal candlestick pattern or indication signal with minimal volume, it may not stay long due to a lack of momentum. A reversal pattern combined with above-average volume is more likely to be sustained.

Breakout Trading Volume Strategy

When a market's price approaches a support or resistance line, it may revert or break out, depending on the strength of the trend. By entering a position as soon as the structure is broken, traders may capitalize on the short-term excitement that frequently occurs when the market exceeds these levels.

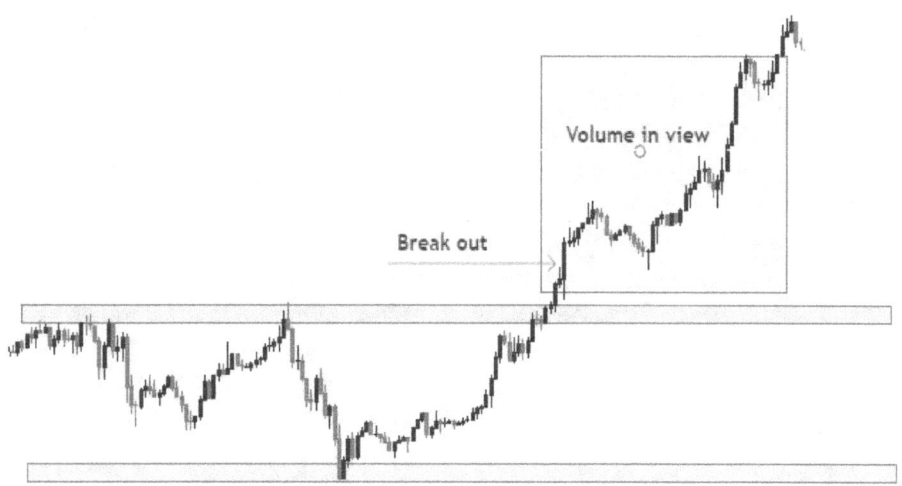

If volume increases during the first breakout, it signals that the new trend is strong. However, no change in volume, or dropping volume, indicates that the price is more likely to retrace.

Because both reversal trading and breakout trading exhibit greater activity around recognized price levels in anticipation of a bigger move, it is critical to employ one or two other indicators for confirmation.

Note: The higher the volume, the safer it is to place an order.

Chapter 3

Introduction to market profile

A market Profile is an advanced charting indicator that shows the total volume traded at each price level during a certain time period. Here's how volume profiles may improve your trading:

1. Determine key support and resistance levels for setups.

2. Set logical take profits and stop losses.

3. Identify balanced and imbalanced markets.

4. Determine trend strength.

Now, let's look at the key components of a market profile:

Market profile components

High and Low Prices

The market profile also offers information on the highest
and lowest prices for a certain time period.

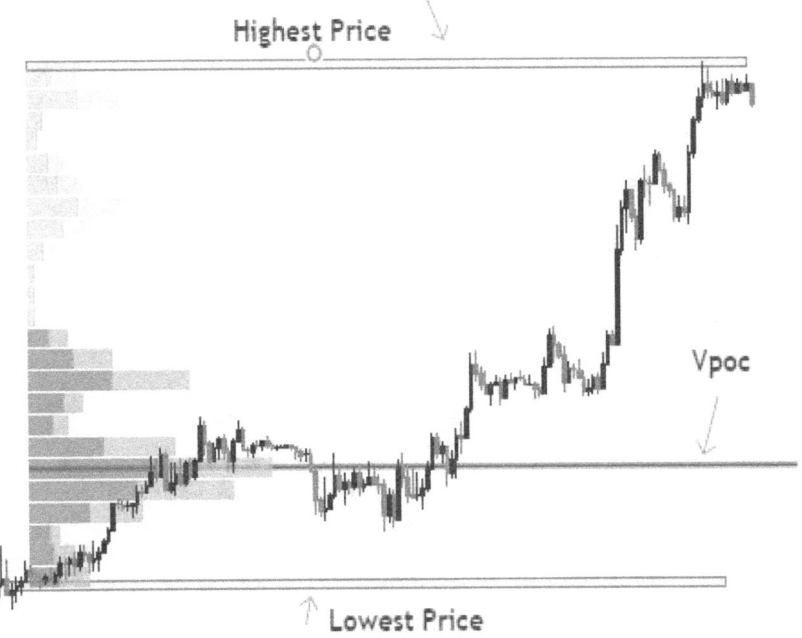

Important of high and low prices level

Trend Identification: The high and low prices assist traders in determining the general trend over a certain time period. Higher highs and lower lows indicate an upward trend, whilst lower highs and lower lows indicate a downward trend.

Breakout Zones: Traders look for probable breakout or breakdown zones in high and low prices. If the market breaks above or below the high or low, it may indicate the beginning of a new trend or a big price change.

Volatility Assessment: The difference between high and low prices offers information on market volatility. Smaller ranges may imply reduce volatility, whereas larger ranges may indicate more volatility.

Volume point of control (VPOC)

The price level with the highest volume transacted during a session, also known as the VPOC. This is the primary reference point I utilize of the market profile.

The Point of Control (VPOC) is an important component of the market profile since it reflects the price level at which the greatest amount of trading activity happened within a certain time period.

Importance of the Vpoc in trading

VPOC because shows a consensus among market players. It implies that a sizable proportion of buyers and sellers discovered value at that particular price level.

Decision-Making Reference

Traders often utilize the VPOC as a point of reference when making trading choices. Trading above the VPOC may indicate positive sentiment, while trading below the VPOC may indicate pessimistic feeling.

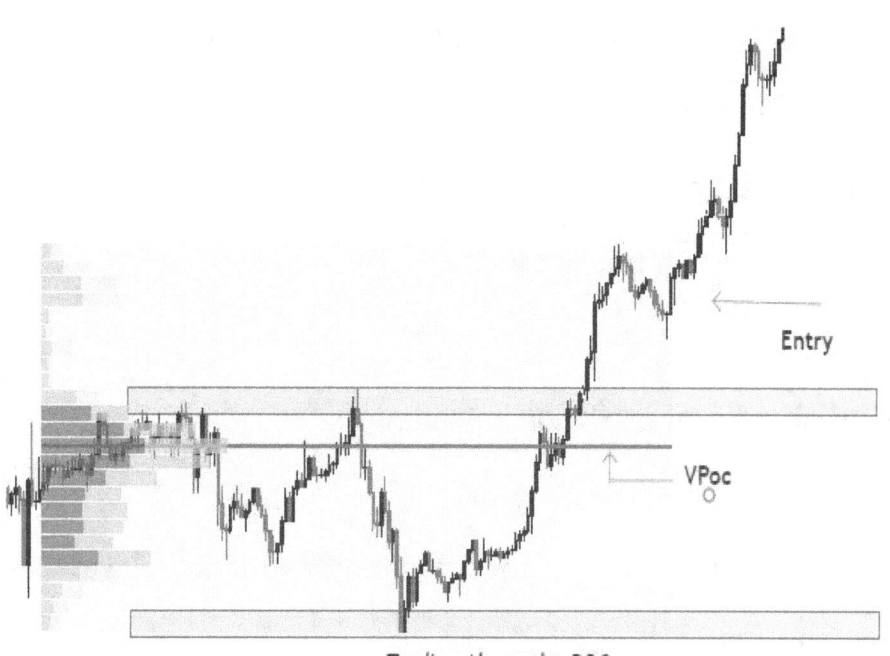

Trading Above the POC

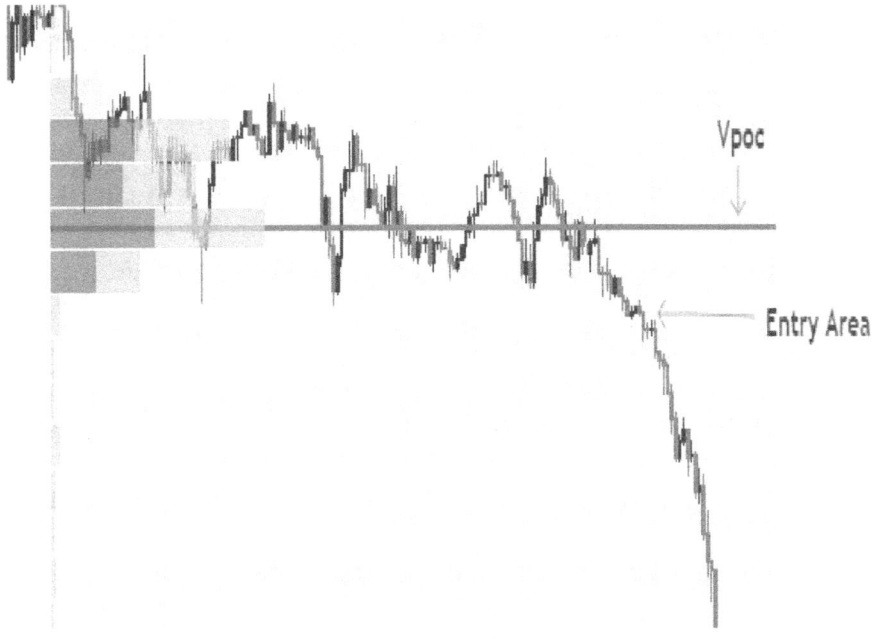

Mean Reversion: Some traders utilize the VPOC as a reference point for mean reversion techniques, believing that prices would drift towards the VPOC over time.

Value Area (VA): The VA is the price range where a certain proportion of volume was traded during a session. Traditionalists often select 70% because it is near to one standard deviation from the mean, as indicated by the Point of Control.

The Value Area is a price range inside a market profile where a certain proportion of total trading activity happened. The most usually used percentage is 70%, however other percentages, such as 80%, may also be utilized.

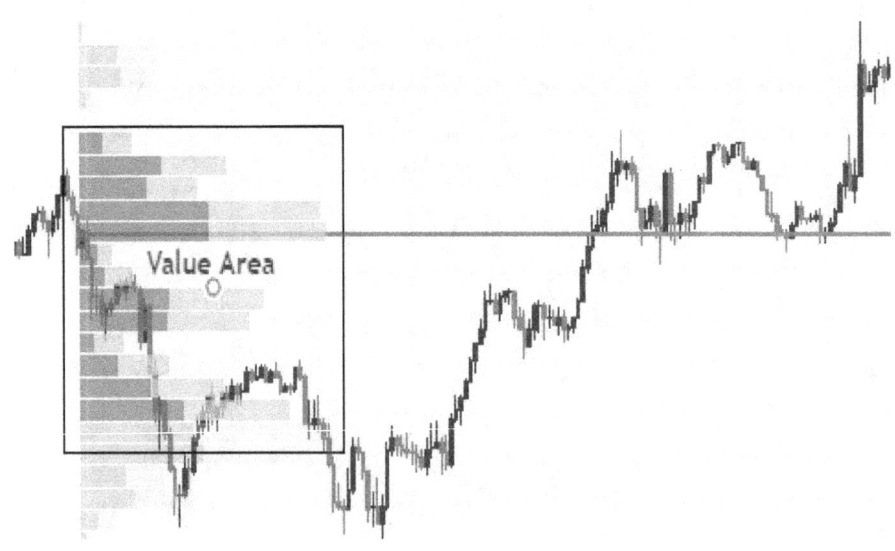

Important of the value area in trading

The computation: The volume distribution is used to determine the Value Area. It includes the price levels where the majority of trade activity took place, showing regions of market acceptability.

Market acceptability: The Value Area indicates the range of acceptability in the market within a certain time period. This areas are very important for future price changes.

Support and Resistance: Traders may view the Value Area's upper and lower bounds as possible support and resistance levels. Price changes outside of this range may indicate a shift in market sentiment.

High Volume Node (HVN): These are regions with more volume than the surrounding price activity.

This is a price level within a market profile that has seen a large amount of trading activity. It denotes a concentration of trading activity at that price.

Significance:

• HVNs are interesting because they identify regions where the market has achieved acceptability. HVNs are often interpreted by traders as areas where buyers and sellers sense value.

• HVNs may serve as possible support or resistance levels. If the market reaches an HVN, traders may anticipate higher trading activity as players respond to the price level's historical importance.

• HVNs are a sign of market memory. Traders use these levels to determine where the market previously discovered value and where major buying or selling have place.

- HVNs are used by certain traders as probable entry or exit opportunities. If the market returns to an HVN and begins to exhibit signals of support or resistance, a trade opportunity may present itself.

Low Volume Node (LVN): These are locations with little volume compared to the surrounding price activity.

Low Volume Node denotes a price level within the market profile with limited trading volume. It denotes regions where the market spent less time or where there was less agreement among participants.

Significance:

- LVNs are often regarded as possible price discovery zones. Because there has been less activity at these levels, they may be more vulnerable to abrupt price fluctuations if the market begins to trade in that region.

Use of the Low Volume Node by traders

• LVNs are watched by traders as possible breakout or breakdown zones. If the market advances confidently through an LVN, it may indicate a change in price movement and the start of a new trend.

• LVNs are segments of the market with less historical recollection. As a consequence, these levels may not provide the same amount of support or resistance as HVNs.

• Traders may see LVNs as markets where prices may shift swiftly. Breakouts from LVNs may be seen as chances to capitalize on early trends.

How to Read Market Profiles

Here are some procedures to take:

Accessing the market profile

Market profile should be available on practically every trading exchange platform. You may also obtain a market profile from your broker or you may choose to access the one on the trading view platform. I will give you a step by step guide on how to access market profile on trading view platform.

Learn the timeframe.

Market profiles use letters and colors to denote the time periods of distinct deals. T hese letters signify time blocks, and based on the information required, you may usually alter the time blocks. For example, the market profile might display you specific deals at 15-minute intervals. Time blocks may be represented by various letters or colors, such as a green 10-minute time block or a letter T for a 30-minute time frame.

Understand the time-price opportunity.

The time-price opportunity, or TPO, is crucial because market profile charts reflect the quantity of trading activity at a certain price level and time of day. This might help you learn more about a possible transaction's worth and follow its price movement from its high to its low, searching for trading patterns to employ in your future trade. Observing price movements in a TPO chart might help you identify the TPOs in your market. Some traders employ both a

TPO and a volume chart, although they serve the same function.

Learn about price volume distribution.

The price volume distribution is a set of data on your market profile chart that shows the amount of volume, or how many transactions happened at particular price ranges. It is critical to understand price volume distribution for your market profile so that you can evaluate how much prices fluctuate during the day and where the majority of deals occur.

Understand the volume.

Volume is a measure of how many deals take place in a certain time period, whether it's a five-minute window or a whole trading day.

The volume of a stock simply indicates how interested other investors are in purchasing or selling it, which may help you estimate the feasibility of certain investments. If you discover that a certain stock has a greater purchase volume before market closing, you might keep it throughout the day before selling it at the last minute to maximize your profits. Market profiles show volume on the x-axis, so keep an eye on how it changes during the day.

Check for the opening price.

Opening price may be a useful chart indicator since it shows the price of the commodity at the start of each trading day. Opening prices may influence a market performance throughout the trading day.

Brief History of Market Profile

Market profile trading, developed by J. Peter Steidlmayer in the 1980s, has grown in favor among institutional and retail traders due to its capacity to provide a more in-depth knowledge of market dynamics.

Market profile trading aggregates price and volume data into a graphical format known as a "market profile chart," which shows the market's price dispersion over time. Traders may use this chart to discover regions of high and weak demand, as well as probable price levels where major trading activity occurs.

Market profile and trading decisions

Market profile trading helps traders make better trading choices by giving useful insights on market movements, risk management, and sentiment. How you may utilize market profiles to make trading decisions:

Identifying market trends:

Market Profile visualizes trading activity and price levels, assisting traders in identifying patterns.

Using the market profile chart, traders may determine whether the market is moving, consolidating, or reversing.

Managing risk:

Market Profile helps manage risk by identifying significant support and resistance levels, as well as locations with heavy trading activity.

Traders may utilize the value area and point of control to determine potential support or resistance levels. This information might be critical for determining stop-loss orders and profit objectives.

Spot Market Sentiment:

Market Profile reveals market sentiment by highlighting areas with high trading activity.

For example, a point of control toward the top end of the Value Area indicates positive mood.

A point of control around the lower end of the Value Area may reflect bearish move.

Practical applications of market profile in trading

Strategic Trade Setups:

Market Profiles provide traders with insights on trading activity distribution, allowing for strategic trade setups.

For instance, a trader may notice a poor low or a poor high formation on the market profile chart.

This happens when the market briefly exceeds the previous day's high or low, but then returns to the Value Area. This scenario may indicate a market reversal, leading traders to place trades anticipating a reversal.

Support and resistance levels:

• Market Profile identifies precise support and resistance levels. The upper and lower bounds of the value region indicate probable price reversals.

By correlating these levels with other technical indicators, traders may make more educated judgments about where to place stop-loss and take-profit orders.

Phases of Consolidation and Breakout

Market profile helps traders discern between times of consolidation and possible breakout.

Trend Identification and Confirmation:

Traders use market profiles to detect developing trends. A constant one-sided distribution of TPOs with a change in point of control indicates a strong and prolonged trend.

Advantages and disadvantages

Advantages:

Market Profile offers a fresh perspective on pricing data and market dynamics.

It provides a clear visual picture of market activity.

Aids in identifying significant levels of support and resistance.

Aids in assessing market mood and probable trend reversals.

Disadvantage:

Market profiles may be complex and may need considerable education.

The interpretations of traders may vary.

In the short terms, it may not be as beneficial for trading.

It works best when paired with other types of analysis.

Chapter 4

Market Profile: Swing Trading Analysis

Using Market Profile, long-term swing trading is a methodical investigation of price movement, volume distribution, and value area over a prolonged time frame. The objective of this strategy is to spot and profit from notable price fluctuations that occur inside the larger market trend.

Swing trading is a trading strategy that aims to profit from short- to medium-term market gains from a few days to several weeks.

How to swing trade using the market profile

Trading strategies and their implementation

Determine Trend Phases:

One of the most important aspects of long-term swing trading using Market Profiles is recognizing trend stages. Identifying different stages in the market trend enables traders to adjust their tactics to the current circumstances.

For swing traders, it is essential to comprehend the characteristics of trending phases. Profiles in a trending market show a pronounced directional bias. A sequence of rising value zones are seen by traders during an uptrend, which suggests ongoing purchasing activity.

Conversely, in downtrends, profiles exhibit lower value regions, demonstrating continuous selling pressure. Traders may validate current trends and modify their positions by identifying these patterns.

Ranging Stages:

The market is not clearly biased in one way or the other during ranging or consolidating moments. Market profiles could have a more evenly distributed value area throughout these stages, and the Point of Control (POC) might stay within a more constrained range. Determining range phases is crucial because it indicates possible shifts in market mood or a brief break in the dominant trend.

Traders might concentrate on shorter-term possibilities and modify their techniques to account for range-bound situations.

Periods of Transition:

For swing traders, the shift from trending to range phases is crucial. When traders identify a market shift, they may modify their methods appropriately. This might include preparing to join fresh positions when indications of a new trend develop or tightening stop-loss levels when a trending phase ends and a range period begins.

Analysis of Trend Strength

For swing traders, determining a trend's strength is crucial. By analyzing the POC's placement and the steepness of value zones, market profiles provide light on a trend's strength. Value zones that are well-defined and extended are often indicative of a strong trend. With this knowledge, traders may assess a trend's possible endurance and decide how best to manage their positions.

Trend Reversal Indicators

For swing traders, spotting possible trend reversals is essential. Early signs of a potential reversal might include variations in the POC, changes in the location of value zones, or the appearance of duplicate distributions.

Traders who are interested in trend reversal indications may utilize these signals to modify their positions, either letting go of transactions to protect gains or getting ready for chances to go countertrend.

Price Action Correlation

The detection of trend phases is improved when price action and Market Profile analysis are correlated. Observing how price behaves around major support/resistance levels and trend-lines in combination with Market Profile patterns offers a more thorough insight. This combined strategy helps traders discern between actual trend developments and simple range price variations.

Identification of Patterns

Identifying patterns in Market Profile is a sophisticated ability that helps long-term swing traders make wise choices. Double distributions, in which a single profile has two different value zones, often indicate changes in market mood and possible trend reversals. P-shaped profiles, which are usual in moving markets, show a significant directional bias, and B-shaped profiles, which are frequently seen during consolidation stages, signal market equilibrium. Through practicing the recognition of these patterns, traders improve their ability to predict shifts in market conditions and take advantage of emerging trends.

Double Distributions

When a single market profile has two different value zones, this is known as double distributions within the profile. This pattern often denotes a change in the mood of the market as well as a possible reversal or continuation of the present trend. Traders that are interested in spotting double distributions might use this knowledge to modify their trading plan, perhaps placing bets in response to the anticipated shift in trend.

B-Shaped or P-Shaped Profiles

For swing traders, it is essential to comprehend the characteristics of B-shaped and P-shaped profiles. A balanced market is indicated by a B-shaped profile, which is often seen during periods of consolidation or indecision.

Conversely, a P-shaped profile, which is often seen in trending markets, indicates a strong directional bias. Traders may better match their strategy to the current state of the market by identifying these trends.

Poor Highs/Lows and Excess

When the market rises swiftly to a high or low but doesn't stay there for very long, it creates poor highs or lows and leaves a gap in the profile. Finding poor highs or lows might provide important details regarding possible reversal zones or places the market could return. Using this information, traders may make more informed decisions and modify their deals as necessary.

Composite Profiles

In order to provide a more thorough picture of market activity, data from many time periods are combined to create composite profiles. Traders may find confluence zones, which highlight the importance of certain price levels, by analyzing how volume and value areas have changed over time. This method improves the trader's capacity to make wise choices by providing a more comprehensive grasp of the market.

For swing traders, finding patterns requires constant learning. A trader's total skill set is improved by consistently honing the capacity to recognize and understand these patterns within Market Profile research, which helps to make more accurate forecasts about the behavior of the markets.

Effective pattern detection helps swing traders make well-timed and knowledgeable judgments at every stage of their trading journey when paired with the more comprehensive examination of Market Profile.

Internal Market Data

When combined with more comprehensive market internals, market profile analysis performs well. Correlations with economic data, other indicators, and market breadth should be observed by traders. Trading choices become more reliable when Market Profile signals are confirmed with more extensive market internals. Confirmation of volume is important; larger volumes indicate important levels of support or resistance or support breakouts. Sentiment analysis is another essential component that measures the mood of market players.

Severe sentiment levels have the ability to serve as contrarian indicators, assisting traders in timing their entry or exits. Long-term swing traders are certain to have a comprehensive awareness of market circumstances according to this all-encompassing methodology.

In fact, swing traders use Market Profiles to find and seize possible market swing opportunities over extended periods of time. A strategic procedure is involved in swing trading using Market Profiles:

Correlation with Broader Market Breadth

The number of rising versus dropping equities in the market is referred to as market breadth. Correlating Market Profile research with market breadth indicators, such as the Advance-Decline Line (ADL) or the McClellan Oscillator, may give a more thorough assessment of overall market health.

Disparities in market sentiment or impending trend changes might be indicated by differences between market internals and Market Profile patterns.

Confirmation of Volume

The Market Profile's volume analysis is improved when it is supported with more comprehensive volume indicators. Increased volume at critical support and resistance levels or during breakouts lends credence to the projected changes in the market. Volume confirmation gives swing traders more confidence by confirming the accuracy of Market Profile signals and assisting them in determining the potential strength of a trend.

Sentiment Analysis

Sentiment research, which measures the disposition of market players, is included into Market Profile trading tactics. Utilizing sentiment indicators, such as the put/call ratio or polls of institutional and retail opinion, helps swing traders to determine whether the market is unduly optimistic or negative. Severe sentiment levels may serve as contrarian indicators, helping traders timing their inputs and exits according to the chance of a sentiment-driven reversal.

Events and Economic Indicators

It is important to integrate Market Profile study with significant economic indicators and events. Economic announcements, like GDP figures or job statistics, may affect the mood of the market as a whole.

Swing traders should be mindful of the economic calendar and modify their holdings as necessary to reduce the risk of unanticipated market-moving events.

Analysis of Inter-markets

Analyzing alternative financial markets, including those for bonds, currencies, or commodities, might provide insightful information. Swing traders may benefit from inter-market research by learning about possible connections between various asset classes and more general market patterns. Understanding inter-market linkages enables traders to operate with more knowledge, particularly when events in linked markets may have an effect on the assets they are trading.

Analysis of Market Structure

Analyzing the behavior of different market players, such as institutional traders and retail investors, is necessary to understand the overall structure of the market. Price fluctuations may be impacted by modifications to the market structure, such as changes in the order flow or the entry of new competitors. Combining market structure research with market profile enables swing traders to adjust to changing market circumstances.

Examine Longer-Term Market Profiles

Analysis of longer-term Market Profiles is extremely useful for swing traders looking to find lucrative chances, especially on weekly or monthly timescales.

These longer periods provide a thorough summary of volume distribution, price fluctuations, and important levels that might influence the course of the market going forward. The basis for well-informed decision-making is laid by traders' ability to recognize dominant trends, probable support and resistance areas, and overall market mood by looking at the longer-term profiles.

The macroeconomic environment of the market may be grasped by traders via the analysis of weekly or monthly profiles. Understanding fundamental changes in the market, differentiating between ranges and trending conditions, and identifying the possibility of large swing moves are all made easier by the newfound knowledge. By using a comprehensive approach, swing traders may better match their tactics with the overall dynamics of the market, increasing the likelihood of profitable transactions.

Levels of Resistance and Support

Longer-term market profiles show important levels of resistance and support that have the power to influence market dynamics. The profiles' peaks and troughs provide light on previous price points that saw a lot of buying or selling activity. Understanding these levels enables traders to set up calculated entry and exit points and modify their risk-reduction plans appropriately.

Analysis of Volume

Swing traders benefit from volume analysis in longer-term profiles since it helps them gauge the strength of price fluctuations. Within the profiles, high-volume nodes often serve as strong zones of resistance or support.

Volume distribution analysis over a longer time span is useful for traders to validate trends and find possible reversal zones.

Point of Control Movement (POC)

For swing traders, it is essential to examine how the Point of Control moves within longer-term profiles. A moving POC might be a sign of altering supply-demand imbalances and modifications to market dynamics. With this knowledge, traders may prepare for future trend continuations or reversals and modify their trading tactics appropriately.

Analyzing Historical Volatility

Longer-term Market Profiles with an analysis of past volatility might assist traders in estimating the possible size of future price changes. Extended periods of high volatility may indicate possible trend fatigue, whereas periods of low volatility may presage notable breakouts. A trader may more successfully manage risk and establish realistic profit objectives when they have a thorough understanding of past volatility.

Examining Seasonal Trends

Examining previous seasonal trends is a necessary step in analyzing longer-term market profiles. At certain points in the year, certain markets could display recurrent patterns. By being aware of these periodic trends, swing traders may modify their approach to take advantage of past trends and project future moves in the market.

Longer-term market profile analysis is a thorough procedure that requires a profound comprehension of several market variables.

Analysis Using Multiple Timeframes

Successful long-term swing trading using Market Profile needs a comprehensive strategy incorporating the examination of both intraday and long-term profiles.

Intraday profiles help with entry and exit point optimization by providing detailed information on short-term market movements. In addition, as previously said, long-term profiles provide a broad perspective of the general health and dominant patterns of the industry.

By coordinating these assessments, traders are able to comprehend market behavior more deeply and are better equipped to make timely judgments that take the long- and short-term into account.

Intraday Profiles

Short-term insights into price changes, volume distribution, and value regions may be obtained by looking at intraday Market Profiles. Intraday patterns and possible short-term chances that correlate with the longer-term market trend may be discerned by traders. Swing trade entry and exit locations may be optimized with the use of intraday analysis.

Daily Profiles

A single day's worth of price and volume data are captured in Daily Market Profiles, which provide a more thorough look at market activity. Swing traders may find important support and resistance levels, trend shifts, and possible breakout opportunities by analyzing daily profiles. Longer-term trends and short-term intraday information are balanced in daily profiles.

Week Profiles

Weekly Market Profiles, which summarize a week's worth of trade data, provide a macro perspective. Identifying broad patterns, significant support and resistance areas, and possible changes in market mood all depend on this time span.

Weekly profiles are a common tool used by swing traders to verify the durability of trends shown over shorter periods.

Monthly Profiles

An even wider view may be obtained by looking at monthly Market Profiles, which include a full month's worth of market activity. Swing traders may find important long-term patterns, critical turning moments, and macroeconomic variables affecting the market with the use of monthly profiles. For a trader to have a clear awareness of the larger market situation, this period is crucial.

Aligning Timeframes

For trading choices to be consistent, the analysis of several periods must be aligned. For instance, when a swing trader notices a positive trend in the weekly profile, he or she is more confident in the transaction if the daily or intraday profile also supports the same direction. The entire trading approach is strengthened when there is consistency throughout several periods.

Verification of Trends

Verifying the longevity of recognized patterns is made easier with the use of multiple timeline analysis. A general trend in the weekly or monthly profile could coincide with a trend seen in the daily profile.

Swing traders might feel more confident about the longevity of the chosen market direction when trends are validated across several periods.

Early Trend Reversal Indications

Early warning indicators of possible trend reversals may be found by analyzing shorter periods in addition to longer-term profiles. Patterns or changes that occur before a reversal shown in the weekly or monthly profiles may be seen in intraday or daily profiles. Swing traders are able to quickly modify their positions due to this early notice.

Timeframe Consistency in Volume Patterns

It is crucial to analyze volume trends consistently throughout a variety of time periods. The expected price movement gains credibility if a breakthrough in the daily profile is confirmed by a spike in volume in the weekly profile. A trader's trust in the strength of observed trends is increased when volume patterns exhibit consistency.

Modifying Position Sizing Depending on Timeframe

Traders may modify position size according to the period of their analysis by taking into account the swing trade's duration. While shorter-term transactions generated from daily or intraday profiles may need lower amounts owing to heightened volatility, longer-term bets based on monthly profiles may demand bigger positions.

Identify Changes in the Poc or Value Area

A critical component of utilizing Market Profiles for swing trading is keeping an eye on changes in the Point of Control (POC) and Value Area. The POC denotes the level with the most volume, while the Value Area shows the price range where most trading takes place. Prominent alterations in these characteristics indicate modifications in the attitude of the market and might function as preliminary markers of prospective trend reversals or the birth of new trends.

A movement in the relative strength of buyers and sellers may be indicated by a move in the Value Area toward higher or lower price points.

Traders keep a close eye on these changes since they might provide important insights into how the market is changing. Swing traders strategically position themselves by identifying and understanding these shifts, lining up their transactions with the emerging trends to optimize profit potential.

Importance of the POC Movement

A larger POC shift indicates a concentration of trading activity at higher price points, which might be seen as possible bullish strength. On the other hand, a lower POC would indicate more selling pressure and perhaps bearish bias. Traders keep a careful eye on POC fluctuations to get insight into new trends.

Verification of Volume using Value Area shifts

The credibility of the detected shifts is increased when Value Area movements are confirmed with volume variations. A movement in the value area that is accompanied by a discernible rise in volume indicates high engagement and supports the shift's possible importance. Volume confirmation offers extra confidence in the directional bias shown by the Value Area.

Behavioral Implications of value area changes

It is essential to comprehend how changes in value area may affect behavior. For instance, a time of consolidation or uncertainty may be indicated if the value area narrows, suggesting that market players are in agreement.

On the other hand, a broadening Value Area can indicate more volatility and divergent views among market players.

Enter Trades in the Direction of Shifts

The next stage for swing traders is to execute trades in line with these directional changes once they have identified significant adjustments in the Value Area or POC. Traders may think about going long and awaiting a bullish trend if the Value Area and POC go higher, suggesting more buying activity.

On the other hand, in the event of a downward movement indicating increased selling pressure, short position can be opened in order to profit from a possibly unfavorable market trend.

Trading in line with these changes synchronizes the trader's approach with the mood of the market, increasing the possibility of successful results. This strategy highlights how crucial it is to adjust to shifting circumstances and use the Market Profile research to make quick, well-informed decisions.

Verification of Changes

It's critical to validate the detected movements in the Value Area, or POC, before making a deal. In order to validate that the observed change is consistent with the larger market environment, this confirmation may include examining consistency across a number of time periods. Verifying shifts reduces the possibility of making trades based on erroneous signals.

Clearly Defined Entry Requirements

Setting precise admission requirements is essential to preserving objectivity and discipline. When making trades based on changes in the Value Area or POC, long-term swing traders should establish clear criteria. This might include watching for confirmation from further technical indicators, a breakout from a critical level, or a certain percentage move.

Making Use of other Technical Indicators

Technical indications provide an additional degree of confirmation to the entrance approach. For instance, employing trend-following indicators such as moving averages or momentum oscillators might give further confirmation of the directional bias suggested by movements in the Value Area or POC. Technical indicators improve trade entry accuracy.

When to Make an Entry

When initiating trades based on movements in the POC or Value Area, timing is crucial. When a shift is verified, traders may decide whether to go in right away or wait for a pullback to get a better entry price. The entry time should be in line with the overall trading plan and the amount of risk taken.

Incorporating Price Action Signals

A qualitative element is added to trade entry when price action is analyzed in combination with changes in the Value Area or POC. Additional confirmation of the expected market direction may be obtained from price action cues, such as candlestick patterns or chart formations.

The trader's ability to make decisions is improved when price action analysis and changes in the market profile are combined.

Risk Management and Position Sizing

Successful trade entry depend on choosing the right position size and putting efficient risk management in place. The risk-reward ratio, the size of trading account, and the volatility of the traded instrument are some of the aspects that long-term swing traders should consider when determining the size of their position. Clearly defining your stop-loss boundaries helps in risk management.

Scaling In and Scaling Out

When the market begins to move in the desired direction, swing traders could think about scaling into positions. With this strategy, partial positions are opened, and exposure is increased as the trade moves in your favor. Scaling out, on the other hand, entails progressively lowering the position size in order to guarantee profits at certain levels. Scaling techniques provide trade management more adaptability.

Real-Time Monitoring

Real-time transaction monitoring must be done continuously. Swing traders with a long time horizon should be on the lookout for indications that the market is changing more quickly than expected.

Reevaluating the transaction on a regular basis in light of fresh information enables flexible decision-making and prompt positional changes.

Changing Entries in Response to News and Events

When making trades, it's important to be informed about impending news releases or economic occurrences. Considering the possible effect of such occurrences on the market, long-term swing traders should modify their entrance.

By being proactive, you can reduce the risks brought on by unforeseen volatility or news that might move the market.

It takes a mix of technical analysis, risk management, and flexibility to enter trades in the direction of changes in the Value Area or POC.

Long-term swing traders may improve the accuracy and potency of their entry and raise the likelihood of profitable trades over longer periods of time by integrating these subtopics into their trading strategy.

Target Swing Points

Equipped with knowledge from Market Profile research, swing traders deliberately aim for certain swing points within the designated trend direction. Key support/resistance levels, historical price activity, and technical analysis tools are often used to identify these swing points. Capturing significant price fluctuations during the swing trade is the aim.

To identify possible entry and exit positions, traders may use a variety of techniques, including trend-lines, Fibonacci retracements, and chart patterns.

Traders seek to maximize their risk-reward ratios by carefully pinpointing key swing moments, making sure that possible gains exceed possible losses. This methodical technique improves the swing trading strategy's accuracy and raises its overall efficacy.

Making Use of Past Price Information

Finding important swing moments requires analyzing past price data. Charts are used by traders to identify historical market reversal points. Swing points from the past may be used as benchmarks to predict future trends or reversals.

Fibonacci Extensions and Retracements

Fibonacci extensions and retracements are a useful tool for traders to use when identifying possible swing points based on the golden ratio. Fibonacci numbers are useful for determining profit objectives since they often serve as resistance or support. Fibonacci tools may be used by traders to increase the accuracy of their trades.

Analysis of Trend-lines

Potential swing points may be found on price charts by drawing trend-lines. Trend-lines may serve as dynamic support or resistance and provide a visual depiction of the directional bias in the market. The trader's ability to match exits with the prevailing trend is improved by aiming for swing points along trend-lines.

Support and Resistance Areas

Finding areas of support and resistance makes it easier to target swing spots. These zones often develop around pivot points, historical price levels, or regions with significant trading activity. Within these ranges, swing traders deliberately set their profit goals in order to take advantage of any reversals or continuations of trends.

Analysis of Volume Profiles

Targeting swing points connected to high-volume nodes is made easier by analyzing volume characteristics. Volume at certain price points reveals places where the market is really interested. When a volume profile study hints to a possible shift in market dynamics, swing traders can think about aiming for such spots.

Psychological Levels

It is usual practice to take psychological levels into account, such as round numbers or critical pricing levels that terminate in zeros. Orders are often placed by market players around these levels, which boosts activity. Exit tactics are more accurate when swing points around psychological levels are targeted.

Target Adjustment to Market Conditions

Long-term swing traders need to modify their goal levels in response to the state of the market. Whereas shorter-term aims could be more suitable in range markets, traders may lengthen targets in trending markets to catch extended trends. Target adjustments depending on the state of the market are essential for maximizing trading results.

Taking Volatility into Account

It's critical to modify target swing points in response to market volatility. In times of increased volatility, traders could adjust their profit objectives to account for greater market fluctuations. On the other hand, objectives could be changed to reflect more subdued price fluctuations in low-volatility conditions.

Strategies for Leaving Partial Positions

Setting up partial position exit strategies is essential for traders using scaling methods. Establishing precise thresholds or requirements for exiting trades guarantees a methodical strategy for extracting profits while enabling the residual position to benefit from any future gains.

Strategies for Trailing Stops

When trailing stop tactics are used, profits may be secured and the trade can stay open in the case of a strong trend. Trailing stops may be programmed to react dynamically to shifting market circumstances by being placed at a specified percentage or depending on particular technical indicators.

Combining technical research, risk management, and flexibility in response to changing market circumstances is necessary to target swing points. Long-term swing traders may improve the accuracy and potency of their target-setting techniques and increase the likelihood of profitable trade outcomes over longer periods of time by integrating these subtopics into their trading strategy.

Chapter 5

Market Profile: Day Trading Analysis

Forex day trading

Forex day trading is the practice of buying and selling currencies inside a single trading day. At the conclusion of each day, positions are closed and new ones are posted the following day. To profit from market fluctuations, forex day traders buy and sell many currency pairs on the same day, or even multiple times in a single day.

Day trading, also known as intra-day trading, is not for the inexperienced trader because it demands time, effort, attention, and a unique attitude. It requires making quick decisions and executing multiple deals for minimal earnings each time.

It is widely regarded as the polar opposite of most investment strategies, which seek to gain long-term profits from price movements.

Before starting day trading

Before you start day trading forex or any other market, there are a few things you should consider because this trading style require more time on your chart than a buy and hold strategy and it requires more risk management skill.

Among them are the following:

Liquidity

The liquidity of a market is determined by how easy and quick it is to enter and exit it.

High liquidity is essential for day traders because they are likely to execute several trades during the day.

Liquidity refers to a currency pair's capacity to be bought and sold on the forex market without significantly altering its exchange rate. A currency is considered liquid when it can be easily purchased and sold and does not experience substantial changes in its exchange rate.

When attempting to comprehend Forex liquidity, two elements should never be overlooked:

- The most liquid currency pairs are the major ones.
- The uncommon currency combinations are the least liquid.

Variables that contribute to the liquidity in forex trading

A tightening of monetary policy

Changes in global monetary policy affect the foreign exchange rate, which in turn affects liquidity. When a government chooses to extend its monetary policy in order to increase the movement of money across the country, the populace's wages and desires rise.

As a result, the value of the home currency falls, and the exchange rate falls. The causes of this are low interest rates and a rise in the amount of credit available globally.

When the global credit supply expands, more loans and borrowings become available to the public, this has a favorable impact on Forex liquidity.

More money in the hands of traders and investors equals more credit available.

Decreased credit demand worldwide

A drop in worldwide credit demand shows that people have enough money for trading and investing. As a result, they do not require additional credit to invest in the foreign currency market.

This is how a decline in global credit demand leads the Forex market's liquidity to rise. However, if global credit demand rises, it may mean that consumers are unable to invest their money, resulting in reduced liquidity in the Forex market.

Volatility

The volatility of an asset is the rate at which the price fluctuates, is critical for day traders. If there is expected to be substantial volatility during the day, there may be several opportunities for rapid profits owing to market movements.

Forex volatility measures the frequency with which a currency's price changes. The more volatile a currency is, the higher the risk of trading it in the Forex market. On the other hand, if you trade particularly volatile currency pairs, you run the potential of making huge profits.

The primary currency pairs are the least volatile, while the exotic currency pairs are the most volatile.

Factors that contribute to Forex volatility

Variations in interest rates

Interest rate changes influence the volatility of the Forex market. Investors will cut back on their spending in an economy where interest rates rise. As a result, the value of the local currency would plummet significantly, increasing market volatility.

Similarly, lower borrowing rates would encourage customers to spend more because they would have more money to do so. This would boost the market value of the domestic currency and induce price changes, increasing market volatility.

Economic shocks that have an influence on supply and demand

Domestic shocks that may have a detrimental impact on Forex volatility include a change in tax legislation or a sudden surge in oil prices. For example, suppose a country sets significant trade barriers that harm a sizable segment of the population (consumers).

In such a scenario, the number of persons trading on the Forex market will fall, lowering the value of currency pairings and increasing volatility.

Similarly, if domestic economies experience an increase in oil prices as a result of excessive demand, the value of the gulf countries' currencies will rise because they will now be producing more oil and earning more money, causing significant foreign exchange volatility.

Global changes and occurrences

Warfare, natural catastrophes, political elections, and other global events and developments can all have a substantial impact on the volatility of the Forex market.

For example, if a country is holding elections, most traders will not choose to invest in that country's currency because a change in government is viewed as a shift in the nation's political feelings, which may cause volatility in the market.

The volume of trades

An asset's trading volume is a measurement of how frequently it is bought or sold over a given time period. A high transaction volume indicates a high level of interest and can be utilized to predict when to enter and exit the market.

The degree of pressure rises with volume and, depending on a number of factors, may indicate the beginning of a trend.

Using the market profile chart as a guide, day traders and scalpers use this method to make quick trading decisions. A technical analysis tool called market profile helps traders find areas of support and resistance as well as possible market turning points by presenting price, timing, and volume data in an easy-to-understand manner.

Day trading and scalping using market profiles are likewise impacted by the same factors that we took into consideration in the preceding chapter on swing trading.

Market profile day trading

A tool that offers a visual depiction of the trade activity in a particular market is the market profile. It shows the total number of trades made over a given time period at various price points. By evaluating the market profile, day traders can acquire insights into the market's overall sentiment and identify critical support and resistance levels.

Traders use market profile to identify trends and anomalies that may suggest future price changes. To find possible locations of support or resistance, they can, for instance, search for high-volume trading zones, or value areas. Market profile can also be used by traders to spot "poor highs" or "poor lows," or price points when there is a notable disparity between buyers and sellers. These levels may portend a reversal or breakout.

Utilizing the market profile for scalping

Scalping

Is a shorter-term trading method used by traders who want to make money from little changes in price. In order to make modest profits from a number of trades made throughout the day, scalpers usually hold their positions for a few minutes to a few hours. Scalpers can use market profiles to control risk and find chances for short-term trading.

When studying market profile, scalpers could concentrate on locating points of control, or regions with a high concentration of volume or trading activity. In addition, they might search for instances of range extension, or places where the market is trading outside of the range from the previous day, as this might suggest possible breakout chances.

It is noteworthy that rigorous analysis, risk management, and a firm grasp of market dynamics are necessary for both day trading and scalping employing market profile. When making trading selections, traders need also take into account other elements like news developments, market trends, and market liquidity.

Chapter 6

Practical session

Applying Market Profile in trading

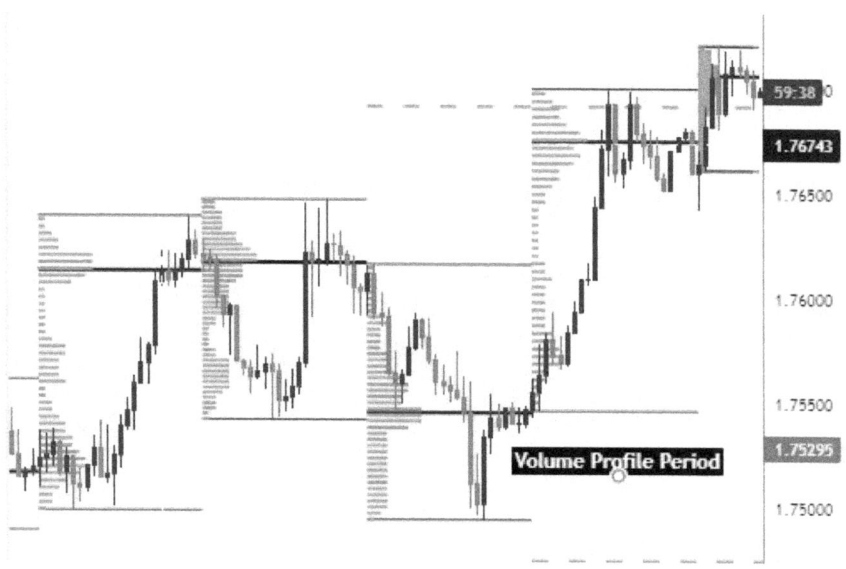

If you look clearly at the above diagram you will discover five different profile covering five different trading days

The diagram summarizes the extensive information presented in the earlier chapters and highlights important concepts like Vpoc, HVD, LVN, etc. It is now time to examine each part in further detail.

There's no reason to worry if this explanation leaves some of the concepts unclear. An extensive video presentation on market profile and how to use it best for swing, day, and scalp trading is included with this course.

Diagrams explaining previous and current day profile

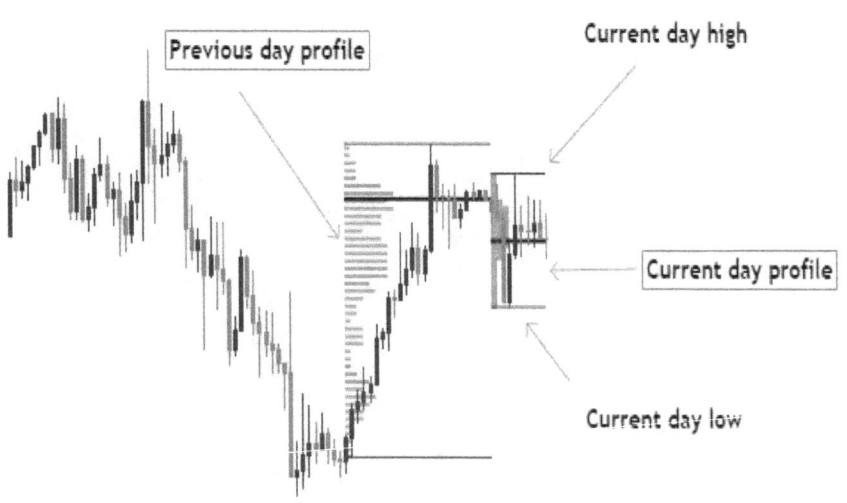

Practical Explanation of value area (Vpoc)

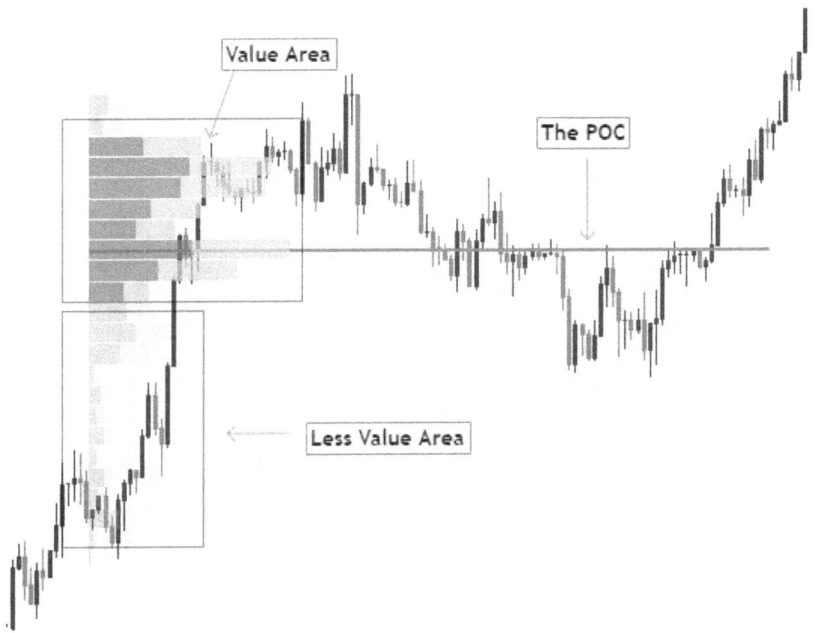

The price level at which the most trading volume happened within a given time period, like a trading session or a predetermined window of time, is known as the Volume Point of Control, or VPOC.

The VPOC can be found by looking for the highest peak on the volume distribution histogram. The reason VPOC matters is that it shows the areas with the highest buying or selling activity, which may indicate future support or resistance.

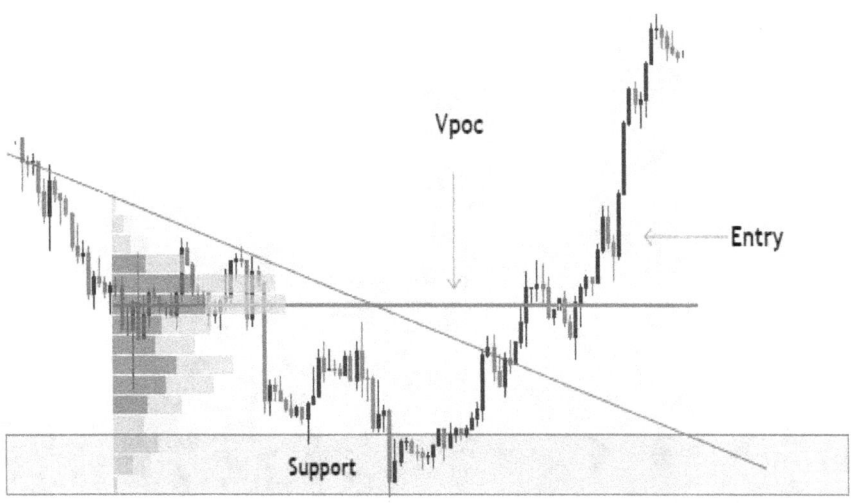

VPOC entry Strategy using break and retest of major support and resistance level

Considering important support and resistance levels near the Volume Point of Control (VPOC) is a strategic method commonly used by professional traders before entry a trade.

When deciding on a trade entry, evaluate the VPOC and its proximity to important support or resistance levels. If the VPOC is closely aligned with a key support or resistance level, it strengthens the level's potential relevance.

The notion is that the VPOC, which represents a large volume of trading activity, validates the market's interest at a certain price. When this level coincides with a key support or resistance region, market players become more convinced that this is a critical zone.

Resistance Level
Support Level

Resistance Level
Support Level

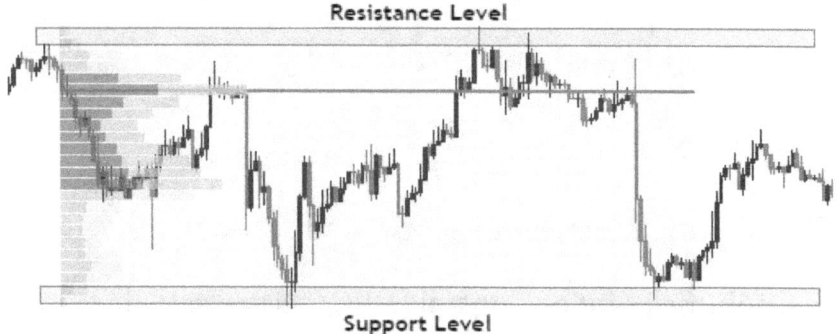

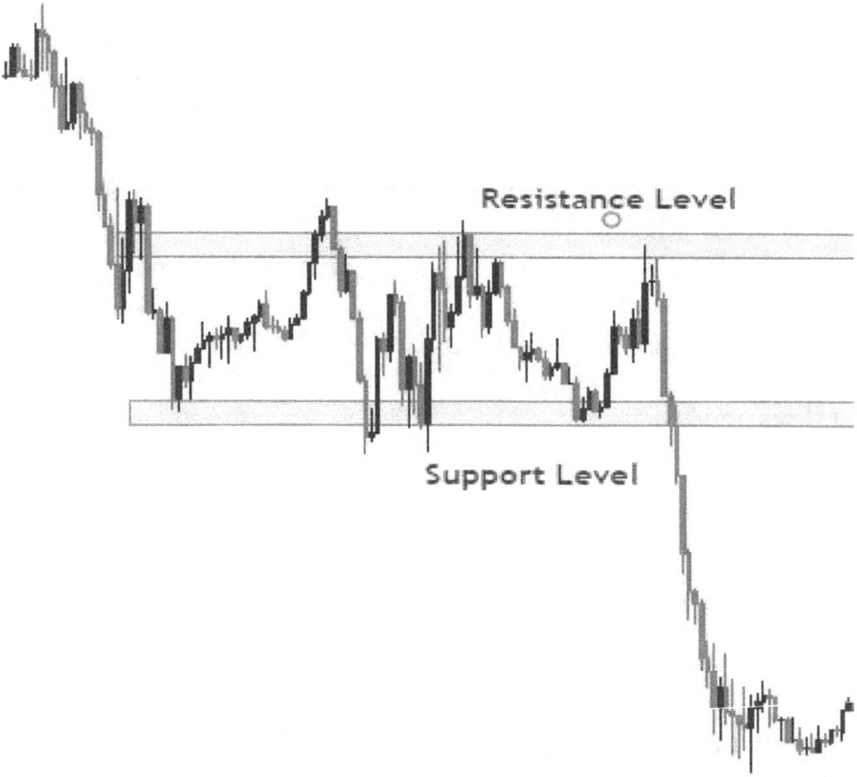

Trading professionals utilize the tactical method of timing an entry when the structure breaks and retests around the Volume Point of Control (VPOC) level in order to profit on probable market reversals or continuations.

Break and Retest the Concept

Waiting for a distinct breakdown of the structure around the VPOC level is the first phase.

This might be a break above or below support, suggesting a possible change in the tone of the market.

Look for a retest of the broken level after the breakthrough. The retest shows that the market is acknowledging the new price level and that the breakout was not a misleading signal.

VPOC Confirmation

VPOC's Influence

The breakout and retest are more significant because of the VPOC's closeness. The market may be reevaluating the value or fair pricing at that level if the breakout happens near to the VPOC.

Verification of Volume

The volume during the breakthrough and retest is something that traders watch closely. An increase in volume throughout these stages demonstrates the market's interest in and dedication to the new market direction.

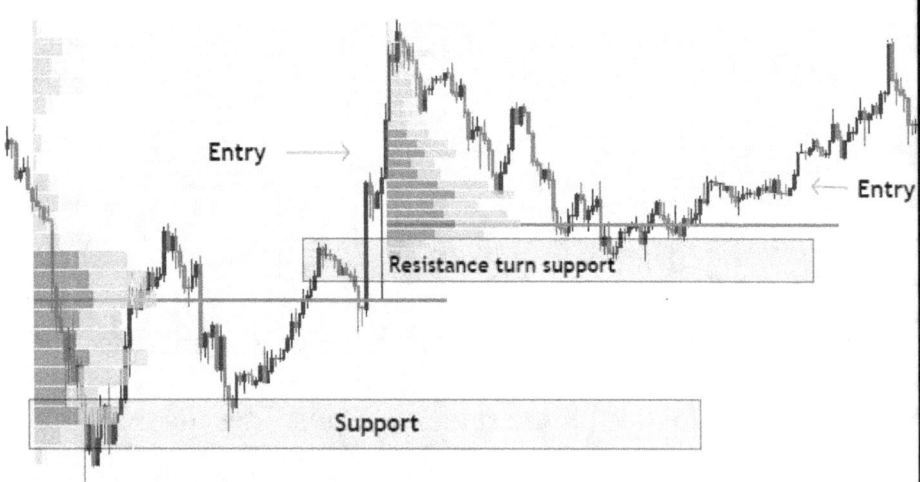

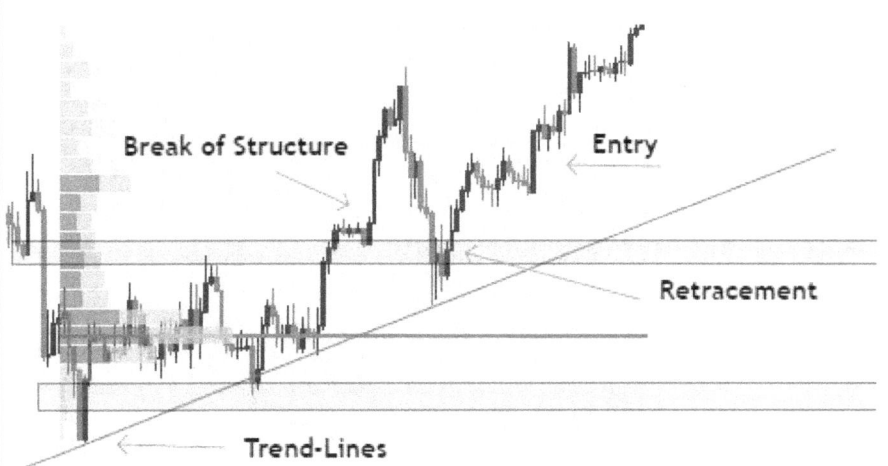

How to locate market profile chat on trading-view platform

Go to trading-view official website

To access a chart, sign in to your Trading-View account with your Gmail and select the market that interests you.

To view the indicators, click the "Indicators" button located at the top of the chart.

Look for "Market Profile" by typing the term into the search box that displays. The Market Profile indicator could exist in several forms, including some specially written scripts made by the Trading-View community.

A subset of the market profile known as the Volume Profile may appear.

Choose the Indicator: The Market Profile indicator should appear on your chart when you click on it to utilize it.

After the Market Profile is shown on your chart, you can often make changes to it by selecting the settings icon that shows up when your cursor is over the indicator name. This is where you may change several characteristics, such color and the range of data it covers.

Check video course attach to this book for more explanation

CONCLUSION

Finally, Market Profile, which focuses on the link between price, volume, and time, is an effective tool for analyzing market activity. Time Price Opportunities (TPOs), which emphasize certain price ranges across time; the Value Area, which represents the generally recognized price range; and the Point of Control (POC), which indicates a balance between buyers and sellers, are its main constituents. This approach gives traders the ability to recognize trends, control risks, and comprehend market mood.

The profile is only a creative and astute method of studying the Forex market.

A trader may learn a great deal about the underlying structure and strength of the market from the Market Profile theories, in contrast to typical technical analysis and charting methods that simply use technical indicators to monitor price changes. A Forex trader may learn a great deal about market activity and the variables influencing it by utilizing the profile's power.

Volume Profile Trading Video Access Link:

https://www.youtube.com/playlist?list=PLsr29W8GhQK2UNk6zBLnG6FPB-84RUdkQ

Other video links:

subscribepage.io/freeforexcourse